THIS LAND CALLED AMERICA: NEW HAMPSHIRE

D1518449

CREATIVE EDUCATION

Published by Creative Education
P.O. Box 227, Mankato, Minnesota 56002
Creative Education is an imprint of The Creative Company
www.thecreativecompany.us

Design by Blue Design (www.bluedes.com)
Art direction by Rita Marshall
Book production by The Design Lab
Printed in the United States of America

Photographs by Alamy (Mike Briner, Classic Image, Mark Goodreau, Andre
Jenny, The Print Collector, Philip Scalia, Tom Till, Frank Vetere), Corbis
(Bettmann, Kevin Fleming, Christopher J. Morris, David Muench, Lee Snider/
Photo Images, Paul A. Souders), Dreamstime (Lightdreamer), Getty Images
(NASA), iStockphoto (Richard Goerg, Robert Manley)

Library of Congress Cataloging-in-Publication Data
Wimmer, Teresa, 1975–
New Hampshire / by Teresa Wimmer.
p. cm. — (This land called America)
Includes bibliographical references and index.
ISBN 978-1-58341-782-9
1. New Hampshire—Juvenile literature. I. Title. II. Series.
F34.3.W56 2009
974.2—dc22   2008009511

First Edition
9 8 7 6 5 4 3 2 1

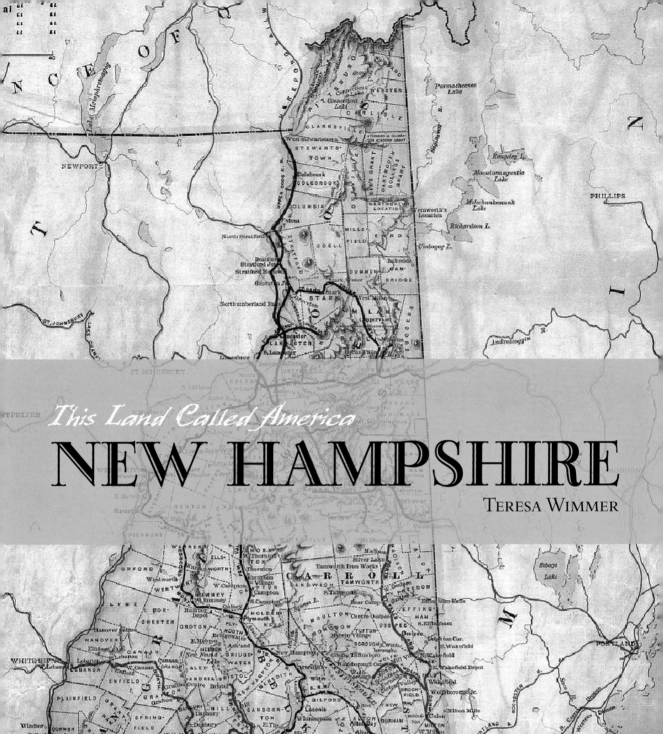

This Land Called America

NEW HAMPSHIRE

Teresa Wimmer

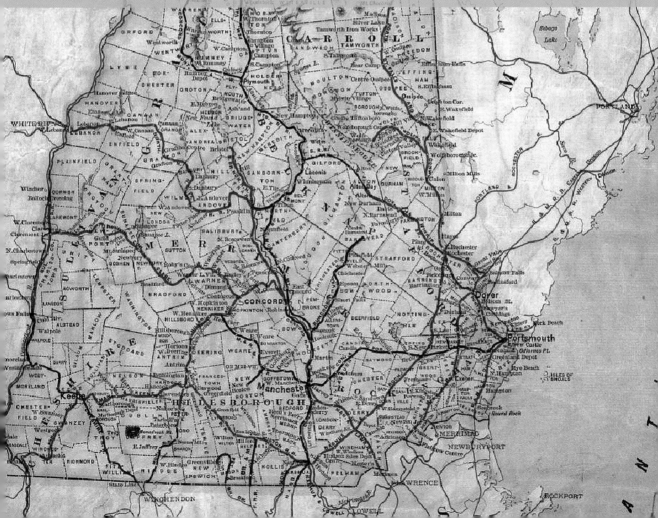

New Hampshire

TERESA WIMMER

ON A WARM SPRING DAY, PEOPLE WALK ALONG A TRAIL AT THE FOOT OF THE SCENIC WHITE MOUNTAINS. THEY PASS GREEN GRASSLANDS DOTTED WITH PURPLE AND YELLOW WILDFLOWERS. NEAR THE TOP, WHERE THE SNOW REMAINS YEAR-ROUND, BRAVE SKIERS SWOOSH DOWN THE SLOPES. THEY WHIZ PAST EVERGREEN PINES AND PAST HARDWOOD TREES JUST BEGINNING TO BUD. SOMETIMES THE WINDS CAN BE HARSH, BUT TODAY THEY ARE CALM. WHEN THE SKIERS STOP TO TAKE A BREAK, THEY GAZE AT THE RUGGED PEAKS THAT SURROUND THEM AND LOOK DOWN ON THE LAKES AND FIELDS BELOW. THEY CANNOT WAIT TO TAKE ANOTHER RUN DOWN THE SLOPES.

YEAR

1614 Englishman John Smith claims New Hampshire for England.

EVENT

Spirit of Independence

HUNDREDS OF YEARS AGO, THE LAND OF NEW
HAMPSHIRE WAS COVERED BY LUSH, GREEN FORESTS.
AMERICAN INDIAN PEOPLE CALLED THE ABENAKI
CUT PATHS THROUGH THE FORESTS. THEY HUNTED
DEER, GREW CORN, AND FISHED IN THE MANY RIVERS
AND STREAMS.

In the early 1600s, men from England and France landed on New Hampshire's coast and sailed up the Piscataqua River, but they did not stay for long. In 1614, Englishman John Smith landed in New Hampshire and claimed the land for England. Soon afterward, many English settlers followed him there.

At first, the Abenaki welcomed the English settlers. They traded furs and land to the English for clothes, metals, knives, and iron pots. But the English people also brought diseases such as smallpox that the Abenaki were not used to. Within a few years, many Abenaki had died from these diseases.

In 1622, the English government gave an Englishman named John Mason a region of land in North America. Mason named his land New Hampshire, after Hampshire, his native county in England. The people of New Hampshire could not agree on one form of government, so in 1641 they chose to become part of the Massachusetts Bay Colony to New Hampshire's south.

After Captain John Smith's (above) arrival in New Hampshire, whites and American Indians fished, hunted, and lived as neighbors for a time (opposite).

YEAR

1641   New Hampshire becomes part of the Massachusetts Bay Colony.

EVENT

- 7 -

In 1679, the English government declared New Hampshire an independent colony, but it did not officially set New Hampshire's borders. This kept people from wanting to buy land in New Hampshire. They did not know if their land would be considered part of New Hampshire or the Massachusetts colony. People also stayed away because of the ongoing fighting in the area between the French and English.

But in the mid-1700s, people began to move to New Hampshire. More English settlers came and founded villages. Other people from Scotland and Ireland came to farm the fertile land in the Connecticut River Valley. They brought a new crop with them called the potato.

New Hampshire's small villages slowly grew into prosperous towns. Mills were built to make cloth. Trees were turned into lumber to make ships. The shipyards in the town of Portsmouth were home to ships that traded with the West Indies, islands far to New Hampshire's south in the Caribbean Sea. The trade made many of Portsmouth's sea captains rich.

In the late 1700s, the 13 American colonies, including New Hampshire, fought for and won their freedom from England. In 1776, New Hampshire became the first colony to have its own constitution. Then, on June 21, 1788, New Hampshire became the ninth state to join the new United States.

The Portsmouth dockyard was a bustling place in the 1880s, with ships being built and repaired there.

YEAR

1679   New Hampshire gains its independence from Massachusetts and becomes a separate colony.

EVENT

- 9 -

In the 1800s, the rich land along the Merrimack and Connecticut rivers lured farmers to the western part of the state. But the soil in the rest of New Hampshire was rocky and not good for farming. Once the farmland was gone, many newcomers moved to the state's cities to work in factories. Paper and textile mills sprang up. Factories churned out shoes, leather goods, bricks, and railroad cars.

During the late 1800s, New Hampshire's cities grew and thrived. Immigrants from countries such as Poland, Italy, Germany, Greece, and Russia moved to New Hampshire. They brought the customs and foods of their homelands with them. By 1900, New Hampshire was home to about 400,000 people from around the world.

Women, men, and even children worked at textile mills in the early 1900s (above), and by the 1940s, women had begun working in sawmills, too (opposite).

YEAR

1690   The English warship *The Falkland* becomes the first important ship built at the Portsmouth shipyard.

EVENT

Big Mountains and Small Towns

New Hampshire lies in the northeastern part of the U.S. in a region known as New England. To the east, it is bordered by Maine. To the north is Quebec, Canada. Vermont lies to the west, across the Connecticut River, and Massachusetts lies to the south. New Hampshire's southeastern corner touches the Atlantic Ocean.

Even though New Hampshire has many modern factories and industries, 85 percent of its land is still covered by trees such as pine, spruce, maple, beech, and balsam fir. Each fall, hardwood trees such as maples and beeches are ablaze with red, orange, and gold colors. Deer, raccoons, beavers, elk, black bears, coyotes, and even moose roam freely through New Hampshire's woods. Much of the forestland is protected by state parks. The largest is Pisgah State Park near Winchester. It contains more than 13,300 acres (5,382 ha) of wilderness paradise.

New Hampshire's land is divided into three main regions: the White Mountains in the north, the Eastern New England Upland in the west and south, and the Coastal Lowlands in the southeast. The White Mountains and their many peaks were named for the snow that tops them even in the summer. One of the peaks is named Mount Washington. It rises to 6,288 feet (1,917 m) and is the highest point in the state. Mount Washington has some of the most dangerous weather in the country. On many winter days, hurricane-force winds gust above 100 miles (160 km) per hour there.

From its rocky shores (opposite) to the snow-covered White Mountains (above), New Hampshire has an abundance of stone.

YEAR

1719 The first potato in the U.S. is planted at New Hampshire's Londonderry Common Field.

EVENT

To the south of the White Mountains lies a region filled with many lakes and small rivers. The rivers and streams teem with fish such as trout, bass, pickerel, and perch. The largest lake in the state is Lake Winnipesaukee. It covers 72 square miles (186 sq km) and contains 274 small islands. The state's longest river, the Connecticut, flows along New Hampshire's western border with Vermont. It helps channel water from the northern mountains to the rivers and lakes of the southern region.

The Eastern New England Upland region is dotted with small towns and farms. The valleys of the Connecticut and Merrimack rivers provide good soil in which farmers can grow hay and vegetables. Many farmers raise animals such as dairy cows, poultry, and hogs. Apple orchards and berry patches are also scattered throughout the region.

New Hampshire's many small villages give people room to spread out (opposite), and its lakes, such as Winnipesaukee (above), offer great views and opportunities for recreation.

The *New Hampshire Gazette* begins publication in Portsmouth.

In Portsmouth, on the border with Maine, fishermen still take their boats out on the ocean every day.

The Coastal Lowlands of the southeast are marked by flat, moist land, a few state parks, and some of the state's oldest cities, such as Portsmouth and Dover. The ocean waters nearby are filled with lobsters, oysters, and clams. Salmon swim up the region's rivers. Important harbors, such as those in Portsmouth, lie along the 18 miles (29 km) of sandy Atlantic coastline.

Because New Hampshire is one of the northernmost states in the U.S., its winters are long, snowy, and cold. Each year, the state gets about 42 inches (107 cm) of precipitation, which includes rain and snow. In the winter, the temperature averages about 20 °F (-7 °C) statewide. Summers are mild with low humidity because cooling lake and ocean breezes sweep across the state. But sometimes those breezes become big summer storms that can turn a pleasant day into a rainy, thunderous one.

Salmon live in the ocean but swim back to the freshwater streams where they were born to give birth.

YEAR

1788   New Hampshire becomes America's ninth state on June 21.

EVENT

- 17 -

Growing and Changing

THE FIRST PEOPLE THAT THE ABENAKI INDIANS OF NEW HAMPSHIRE GREETED WERE ENGLISH SETTLERS. LATER, PEOPLE FROM POLAND, GERMANY, ITALY, GREECE, HUNGARY, AND SCANDINAVIA CAME TO FARM THE LAND AND WORK IN FACTORIES. FRENCH-SPEAKING PEOPLE FROM QUEBEC, CANADA, ALSO TRAVELED TO NEW

Visitors enjoy New Hampshire's natural scenery at resorts in Waterville Valley.

Hampshire to make their homes there. Through the years, French-Canadian immigrants managed to preserve their language and culture in a new land. Today, 25 percent of New Hampshire's residents are of French-Canadian ancestry.

New Hampshire claims residents from most ethnic backgrounds, but 95 percent of its people are white. People of African American, Asian, and Hispanic descent make up small percentages of the population. About half of New Hampshire's population of 1.3 million lives in cities, and half lives in rural areas. Manchester is the largest city in New Hampshire, but it has only about 100,000 people. Because the state is not crowded, most people have easy access to peaceful wilderness retreats.

Manchester is the industrial center of the state and a site where many mills were built.

YEAR

1833 The first public library in the U.S. is founded in Peterborough.

EVENT

The childhood home of Franklin Pierce, the 14th U.S. president, was built in 1804 in Hillsborough.

The beautiful wilderness and countryside have inspired many of New Hampshire's artists and writers through the years. The southern town of Peterborough is home to the MacDowell Colony, a 450-acre (182 ha) retreat for artists, writers, and composers. Twentieth-century composer Leonard Bernstein wrote some of his best music while living there. Playwright Thornton Wilder was also a MacDowell guest. In 1938, Wilder wrote his famous play *Our Town*, which was based on the town of Peterborough.

Today, less than one percent of New Hampshire's residents farm, but the state remains a leading producer of vegetables, apples, strawberries, and raspberries. Maple syrup from the forests is also famous throughout the world. While New Hampshire's shoreline may be short, its waters provide at least 5,000 tons (4,536 t) of flounder, cod, and lobster every year.

YEAR

1853   Franklin Pierce of Hillsborough becomes the 14th president of the U.S.

EVENT

*After sap is collected, it
is boiled down to make
syrup in sap houses, also
called "sugar shacks."*

Because New Hampshire has few natural resources and mainly rocky farmland outside of the Uplands region, people turned to manufacturing in the 1800s, which gave way to the scientific industries of the late 1900s. Many New Hampshire residents make high-tech goods such as electronics, hospital equipment, and computers. Others work in factories that make boots and lamps. Food processing of products such as soft drinks and frozen vegetables is also a major industry. Many people work as doctors, teachers, government employees, or in restaurants. Others work in the tourism or logging industries.

New Hampshire has managed to preserve its natural spaces while promoting technological advancements. The state helped launch the U.S. into the space age on May 5, 1961. On that date, astronaut Alan Shepard Jr., who was born in East Derry, rocketed away from Earth in a tiny space capsule called *Freedom 7*. His flight marked the first time the U.S. had put a man into space.

Alan Shepard's historic space flight aboard the Freedom 7 *capsule (above) lasted a little over 15 minutes.*

Lumberjacks use heavy machinery to transport huge logs, which have to be secured together with chains.

YEAR
1869   The world's first cog railway is built to climb Mount Washington.
EVENT

- 23 -

The Wentworth

Ⅰn the mid-1900s, people from Massachusetts began to move to New Hampshire to escape their crowded cities. They chose to live mainly in southern cities such as Derry, Nashua, Manchester, and Hampton. Many found work in the new scientific and high-tech industries. These newcomers have caused the state's population to more than double since 1950.

The influx of new residents, high-tech businesses, and tourism has given New Hampshire residents one of the highest standards of living in the country. People there enjoy quality hospitals, schools, and job opportunities. The state also has a low crime rate.

Elegant inns may not often be distinguished for their architecture (above), but the library at Hanover's Dartmouth College (opposite) is a copy of Philadelphia's famous Independence Hall.

YEAR

1918 White Mountain National Forest is created and quickly draws many outdoor enthusiasts.

EVENT

Postcard Perfect

THOUSANDS OF YEARS AGO, BIG SHEETS OF ICE CALLED
GLACIERS MOVED OVER NEW HAMPSHIRE. THEY WORE
DOWN MUCH OF THE LAND, BUT THEY LEFT BEHIND TALL,
ISOLATED HILLS CALLED MONADNOCKS (*MUH-NAD-NOCKS*).
THE ROCKY HILLS WERE TOO HARD TO BE WORN DOWN
BY GLACIERS. THE HIGHEST IS MOUNT MONADNOCK IN
SOUTHWESTERN NEW HAMPSHIRE. IT IS 3,165 FEET (965 M)

tall. People come from all over the country to hike its steep, rough slopes.

The White Mountains are also a favorite destination for sightseers. Granite forms the bedrock for many of these mountains. That is why New Hampshire is nicknamed "The Granite State." Each year, thousands of people ride the cog railway to the top of Mount Washington. The railway, which was built in 1869, uses special wheels to climb the mountain's steep slopes. After the one-and-a-half-hour ride to the top, visitors are rewarded with a breathtaking view that allows them to see four different states.

The White Mountains are home to a number of small, beautiful towns as well. Wildflower fields, church steeples, and quaint brick buildings mark the landscapes of these towns. Winter scenes from many towns are put on postcards that are sold worldwide. The state's many covered bridges are also often pictured. The western town of Cornish is home to one of the longest wooden covered bridges in the country.

Some of the state's covered bridges have been preserved in state parks near the White Mountains.

The rough outcroppings of granite can make climbing Mounts Washington and Adams difficult (opposite).

YEAR

1964   New Hampshire is the first state in the 20th century to legalize a statewide lottery.

EVENT

- 27 -

Many open-air rooms and walls make up the structure known as America's Stonehenge.

The history of most of New Hampshire's covered bridges is well-documented, but at North Salem in the southeastern corner of the state stands a stone structure that baffles scientists. The structure is called America's Stonehenge because it looks like the famous Stonehenge in England. It is made of stone blocks that weigh up to 10 tons (9 t) and are arranged in a circle. No one knows who built the structure or why, but tools found at the site are thought to be 4,000 years old. Some people believe that America's Stonehenge was used to chart the movement of the sun and moon. Today, hundreds of people visit this mysterious ruin every day.

Among other popular tourist attractions in New Hampshire are the Isles of Shoals, a group of 9 small islands located 10 miles (16 km) off the coast. Four of the islands belong to New Hampshire, and the other five belong to Maine. Legend says that the famous pirate Blackbeard buried treasure on

The White Island Light was the first lighthouse established on the Isles of Shoals in 1821.

QUICK FACTS

Population: 1,315,828

Largest city: Manchester (pop. 108,871)

Capital: Concord

Entered the union: June 21, 1788

Nickname: Granite State

State flower: purple lilac

State bird: purple finch

Size: 9,350 sq mi (24,216 sq km)—46th-biggest in U.S.

Major industries: manufacturing, farming, logging, tourism

one of the islands. Today, thousands of visitors take boat trips to the Shoals. They watch for birds such as thrushes and yellowthroats and marine animals such as whales and harbor seals.

On the opposite side of the state, Hanover, along the Connecticut River, is home to Dartmouth College. The school was founded in 1769 to educate American Indians and is the nation's ninth-oldest college. Sports fans around the state cheer for the Dartmouth College Big Green, the University of New Hampshire Wildcats, and the Can-Am Baseball League's Nashua Pride.

New Hampshire is a beautiful land to anyone who sees it. Visitors come to ski the mountains, marvel at the fall leaves, camp in the forests, and hike the state's many miles of trails. They also come to escape crowded cities and enjoy fresh air. Every day, New Hampshirites welcome them with friendly smiles and eagerly show them all of the Granite State's treasures.

YEAR

2003   The "Old Man of the Mountain," a series of mountain ledges that looked like a face, collapses.

EVENT

- 31 -

BIBLIOGRAPHY

Blanding, Michael, and Alexandra Hall. *Moon Handbooks: New England*. Emeryville, Calif.: Avalon Travel, 2007.

Mobil Travel Guide. *New England 2006*. Lincolnwood, Ill.: ExxonMobil Travel Publications, 2006.

Moehlmann, Kristin, ed. *Fodor's New England*. New York: Random House, 2007.

Morison, Elizabeth Forbes, and Elting E. Morison. *New Hampshire: A Bicentennial History*. New York: W. W. Norton & Company, 1976.

New Hampshire Department of Resources and Economic Development. "Welcome to New Hampshire." State of New Hampshire. http://www.visitnh.gov.

INDEX